Praise the Lord

Publications International, Ltd.

Praise the Lord

Cherish the chance to work and play and think and speak and sing; all simple pleasures are opportunities for grateful praise.

Praise the Lord

O Word of God Incarnate,

O Wisdom from on high,

O Truth unchanged, unchanging,

O Light of our dark sky:

We praise thee for the radiance

That from the hallowed page,

A lantern to our footsteps,

Shines on from age to age.

—"O Word of God Incarnate"

Praise the Lord

Holy Spirit, the life that gives life.

You are the cause of all movement;

You are the breath of all creatures;

You are the salve that purifies our souls;

You are the ointment that heals our wounds;

You are the fire that warms our hearts;

You are the light that guides our feet.

Let all the world praise you.

—Hildegard of Bingen

Praise the Lord

Blessed assurance, Jesus is mine!
Oh what a foretaste of glory divine!
Heir of salvation, purchase of God,
Born of His Spirit, washed in His blood.
Perfect submission, perfect delight!
Visions of rapture now burst on my sight;
Angels descending bring from above
Echoes of mercy, whispers of love.
Perfect submission—all is at rest,
I in my Savior am happy and blest;
Watching and waiting, looking above,
Filled with His goodness, lost in His love.
This is my story, this is my song,
Praising my Savior all the day long;
This is my story, this is my song,
Praising my Savior all the day long.

—Fanny J. Crosby

Praise the Lord

Every moment we are alive is full of reasons to sing out in joyful gratitude. Every breath we are given is a reminder that the glory of life is at hand. In the people we love, in the beauty of nature, in the golden sun that rises each morning—miracles are everywhere.

Praise the Lord

Whate'er my fears or foes suggest,

you are my hope, my joy, my rest.

My heart shall feel your love and raise

my cheerful voice to sing your praise.

—Isaac Watts

Praise the Lord

For the beauty of the earth,

For the glory of the skies;

For the love which from our birth,

Over and around us lies;

Lord of all, to Thee we raise

This, our hymn of grateful praise.

For the joy of human love,

Brother, sister, parent, child;

Friends on Earth and friends above,

For all gentle thoughts and mild;

Lord of all, to Thee we raise

This, our hymn of grateful praise.

—Folliott S. Pierpoint

Praise the Lord

Gratitude is the memory of the heart.

—Jean Baptiste Massieu

I can no other answer make, but,
thanks, and thanks.

—William Shakespeare

Praise the Lord

We cannot in any better manner glorify the Lord and Creator of the universe than that in all things, how small soever they appear to our naked eyes, but which have yet received the gift of life and power of increase, we contemplate the display of his omnificence and perfections with utmost admiration.

—Anton Van Leeuwenhoek

Praise the Lord

We thank you, God,

for the moments of fulfillment:

the end of a day's work,

the harvest of sugar cane,

the birth of a child,

for in these pauses

we feel the rhythm

of the eternal.

—Hawaiian Prayer

Praise the Lord

Jesus, friend of the poor,

Feeder of the hungry,

Healer of the sick,

I adore thee.

—A Book of Prayers for Students

Praise the Lord

Savior, teach me day by day,

Love's sweet lesson to obey;

Sweeter lesson cannot be,

Loving Him Who first loved me.

Teach me thus Thy steps to trace,

Strong to follow in Thy grace,

Learning how to love from Thee,

Loving Him Who first loved me.

Thus may I rejoice to show

That I feel the love I owe;

Singing, till Thy face I see,

Of His love Who first loved me.

—Jane E. Leeson

Praise the Lord

Thanksgiving is nothing if not a glad and reverent lifting of the heart to God in honour and praise for His goodness.

—James R. Miller

Praise the Lord

On our way to rejoicing gladly let us go.

Christ our Lord has conquered; vanquished is the foe.

Christ without, our safety; Christ within, our joy;

who, if we be faithful, can our hope destroy?

On our way rejoicing; as we forward move,

hearken to our praises, O lest God of love!

Unto God the Father joyful songs we sing;

unto God the Savior thankful hearts we bring;

unto God the Spirit bow we and adore,

on our way rejoicing now and evermore.

On our way rejoicing; as we forward move,

hearken to our praises, O blest God of love!

—John S. Monsell

Praise the Lord

We plow the fields and scatter

The good seed on the land,

But it is fed and watered

By God's almighty hand;

He sends the snow in winter,

The warmth to swell the grain,

The breezes and the sunshine,

And soft, refreshing rain.

All good gifts around us

Are sent from heaven above:

Then thank the Lord, O thank the Lord

For all His love.

—Matthias Claudius

Praise the Lord

Be thou my vision, O Lord of my heart;

Naught be all else to me, save that thou art:

Thou my best thought, by day and by night,

Walking or sleeping, thy presence my light.

Riches I heed not, or man's empty praise,

Thou mine inheritance, now and always:

Thou and thou only, first in my heart,

High King of heaven, my treasure thou art.

—"Be Thou My Vision"

Praise the Lord

God passes through the thicket of the world,
and wherever his glance falls he turns all
things to beauty.

—St. John of the Cross

Praise the Lord

When you have no helpers, see all your helpers in God. When you have many helpers, see God in all your helpers. When you have nothing but God, see all in God; when you have everything, see God in everything. Under all conditions, stay thy heart only on the Lord.

—Charles Spurgeon

Praise the Lord

O worship the King, all glorious above,
O gratefully sing His power and His love.

—Robert Grant

Praise the Lord

Blessed and praised be the Lord, from whom comes all the good that we speak and think and do.

—Teresa of Avila

Praise the Lord

This world…is still a miracle; wonderful, inscrutable, magical, and more, to whosoever will think of it.

—Thomas Carlyle

Praise the Lord

When my life-work is ended,

and I cross the swelling tide,

when the bright and glorious

morning I shall see,

I shall know my Redeemer when

I reach the other side,

and his smile will be the first to

welcome me.

Oh, the soul thrilling rapture when I

view his blessed face,

and the luster of his kindly beaming eye!

How my full soul shall praise him for the

mercy, love, and grace

that prepare for me a mansion in the sky.

Through the gates to the city in a robe

of spotless white,

he will lead me where no tears

shall ever fall.

In the glad songs of ages I shall mingle with delight;

but I long to meet my Savior first of all.

—Fanny J. Crosby

Praise the Lord

O spread the tidings 'round, wherever man is found,
wherever human hearts and human woes abound;
let every Christian tongue proclaim the joyful sound:
The Comforter has come!
The Comforter has come, the Comforter has come!
The Holy Ghost from heaven,
the Father's promise given;
O spread the tidings 'round, wherever man is found—
the Comforter has come!
The long, long night is past, the morning breaks at last,
and hushed the dreadful wail and fury of the blast,
as over the golden hills the day advances fast!
The Comforter has come!

—Frank Bottome

Praise the Lord

When I think of God, my heart is so full of joy that the notes leap and dance as they leave my pen: and since God has given me a cheerful heart, I serve him with a cheerful spirit.

—Franz Joseph Haydn

Praise the Lord

Be kind to your little children, Lord.
Be a gentle teacher, patient with our weakness
and stupidity.
And give us the strength and discernment to do
what you tell us,
and so grow in your likeness. May we all live in
the peace that comes from you.
May we journey towards your city, sailing through
the waters of sin
untouched by the waves, borne serenely along by
the Holy Spirit.
Night and day may we give you praise and thanks,
because you have
shown us that all things belong to you, and all
blessings are gifts from you.
To you, the essence of wisdom, the foundation of
truth, be glory for evermore.

—Clement of Alexandria

Praise the Lord

Glorious indeed is the world of God around us,
but more glorious the world of God within us.

—Henry Wadsworth Longfellow